Little Pebble™

Simple Machines
Wedges

by Martha E. H. Rustad

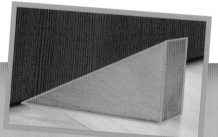

CAPSTONE PRESS
a capstone imprint

Little Pebble is published by Capstone Press,
1710 Roe Crest Drive, North Mankato, Minnesota 56003
www.mycapstone.com

Library of Congress Cataloging-in-Publication Data
Names: Rustad, Martha E. H. (Martha Elizabeth Hillman), 1975– author.
Title: Wedges / by Martha E.H. Rustad.
Description: North Mankato, Minnesota : Capstone Press, 2018. | Series:
     Little pebble. Simple machines | Includes bibliographical references and
     index. | Audience: Ages 4–7.
Identifiers: LCCN 2017031580 (print) | LCCN 2017042206 (ebook) |
     ISBN 9781543500851 (eBook PDF) | ISBN 9781543500738 (hardcover) |
     ISBN 9781543500790 (paperback)
Subjects: LCSH: Wedges—Juvenile literature.
Classification: LCC TJ1201.W44 (ebook) | LCC TJ1201.W44 R87 2018 (print) | DDC
     621.8—dc23
LC record available at https://lccn.loc.gov/2017031580

Editorial Credits
Marissa Kirkman, editor; Kyle Grentz (cover) and Charmaine Whitman (interior), designers;
Jo Miller, media researcher; Katy LaVigne, production specialist

Image Credits
Capstone Studio: Karon Dubke, 13; Dreamstime: Thomas Gowanlock, cover (wood),
1 (wood); Shutterstock: Aleksandar Mijatovic, 19, biggunsband, 24, ffolas, 7, Hans
Christiansson, 11, Kietichal charoentrirat, cover (wedge), 1(wedge), Martin Haas, 15, Monkey
Business Images, 17, Noerenberg, 9, Paradise On Earth, 14, Purino, 5, trekandshoot, 19,
wavebreakmedia, 21

Design Elements
Capstone

Printed and bound in the USA.
010766S18

Table of Contents

Help With Work

Work is hard!

We need help.

Use a simple machine.

These tools help us work.

wedge

A wedge helps us move a load.

It pushes two things apart.

wedge

load

How Wedges Work

Look at the side.

See the triangle.

A wedge has a thin end.

The other end is wide.

Put the thin end here.

Push on the wide end.

The wedge moves.

It splits the two parts.

wedge

Everyday Tools

An ax is a wedge.

Chop!

The log splits.

A doorstop is a wedge.

Slide!

It holds the door open.

CAUTION

WET
FLOOR

15

A knife is a wedge.

Slice!

The bread is cut.

A pushpin is a wedge.

Push!

The paper hangs on the wall.

We use a simple machine.

It makes work easier and fun.

Glossary

knife—a tool with a sharp blade; people use knives to cut things such as food

load—an object that you want to move or lift

simple machine—a tool that makes it easier to do something

split—to break something into two parts

tool—an item used to make work easier

triangle—a shape with three sides

wedge—a simple machine with one thin end and one wide end

work—a job that must be done

Read More

LaMachia, Dawn. *Wedges at Work.* Zoom in on Simple Machines. New York: Enslow Publishing, 2016.

Miller, Tim and Rebecca Sjonger. *Wedges in My Makerspace.* Simple Machines in My Makerspace. New York: Crabtree Publishing, 2017.

Rivera, Andrea. *Wedges.* Simple Machines. Minneapolis: Abdo Zoom, 2017.

Internet Sites

Use FactHound to find Internet sites related to this book.

Visit www.facthound.com

Just type in 9781543500738 and go.

Super-cool stuff!

Check out projects, games and lots more at
www.capstonekids.com

Critical Thinking Questions

1. What shape can you see on the side of a wedge?

2. What happens to the load when a wedge pushes into it?

3. What types of wedges have you used?

Index